BIOENERGY

GRAHAM HOUGHTON

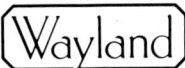

Titles in the series

Bioenergy
Geothermal Energy
Solar Energy
Water Energy
Wind Energy

Cover: *A methane gas producing plant in Ireland.*

Consultant: Dr Mike Flood, PhD

Editor: Paul Mason

Designer: Charles Harford/David Armitage

First published in 1990 by
Wayland (Publishers) Limited
61 Western Road, Hove
East Sussex BN3 1JD, England

© Copyright 1990 Wayland (Publishers) Limited

British Library Cataloguing in Publication Data
Houghton, Graham, *1950* –
  Bioenergy.
  1. Energy sources: Biomass of waste materials
  I. Title II. Series
  662.6

ISBN 1 85210 979 3

Phototypeset by Rachel Gibbs, Wayland
Printed in Italy by G. Canale by C.S.p.A, Turin
Bound in Belgium by Casterman S.A.

Words that appear in the glossary are printed in **bold** type the first time they appear in the text.

Contents

WHY ALTERNATIVE ENERGY?	4
PLANT POWERHOUSES	8
BIOENERGY – THE ANCIENT ALTERNATIVE	10
RELEASING BIOENERGY	14
BIOMASS INTO OTHER FUELS	16
BIOENERGY IN ACTION	24
PROJECT	28
Glossary	30
Further information	31
Books to read	31
Index	32

WHY ALTERNATIVE ENERGY?

Most of the energy we use is produced by burning **fossil fuels** – coal, oil and natural gas. These fuels formed millions of years ago out of the remains of dead plants and animals.

Fossil fuels have served us well for the past 200 years or so, but they have serious disadvantages. For one thing, they are not being made any more. The day will come when the last piece of coal has been burned and the last drop of petrol has been put into someone's fuel tank. Our homes could grow cold. Our factories could stop working. And our

Below *Cars that use petrol, such as these on a busy motorway in California, are using a resource we cannot replace.*

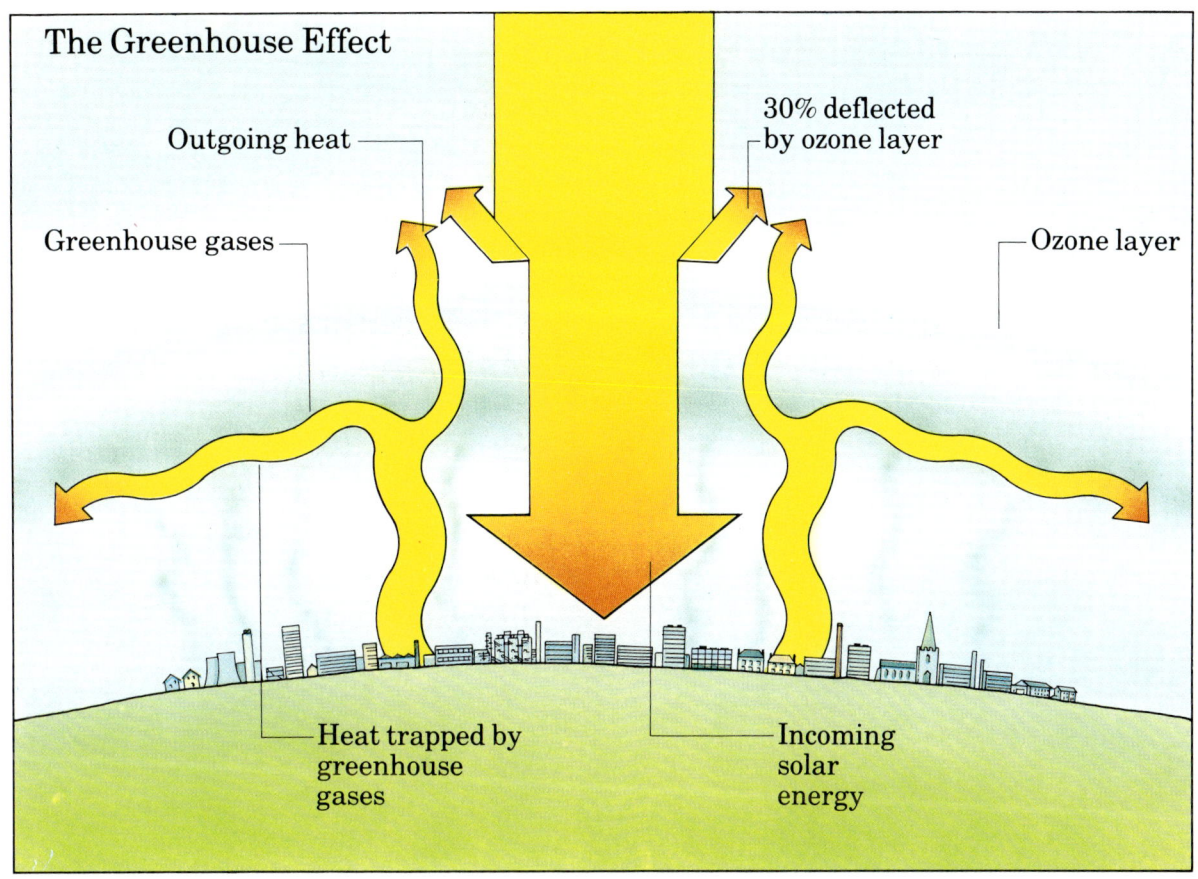

Above *The use of fossil fuels causes the **greenhouse effect**, which leads to warmer weather. This can cause flooding in low-lying areas and drought in warm countries.*

transport could grind to a halt.

As far as oil is concerned, that day might not be more than thirty years away! This is not so surprising when you realize that California in the USA alone uses about a billion gallons of petrol each month. Or that more coal has been burned since the Second World War than in the whole of our former history. The demand for coal grows greater every day, so it is being used up more and more quickly.

Burning fossil fuels creates serious **pollution**. When things burn they release gases into the air. Some of these gases are called **greenhouse gases**. They are called greenhouse gases because they keep the Sun's heat in just as the glass in a greenhouse does. Much of the energy from the Sun that reaches the Earth escapes back into space. Some of it is trapped by the greenhouse gases in the air, though. These gases keep our planet warm enough to live on.

WHY ALTERNATIVE ENERGY?

Above *One effect of burning fosil fuel is to cause acid rain, which strips the leaves from trees and kills fish.*

By burning huge amounts of fossil fuel we are actually increasing the amount of greenhouse gases in the air. This means that more heat is being trapped and the Earth is becoming warmer. This sounds like a good thing, but a change in the climate will do more harm than good. For instance, there may be crop failures due to lack of rain and sea levels may rise as icebergs at the North and South Poles melt.

Other gases are released by burning fossil fuels. These gases dissolve in rain as it falls to the ground and turn the rain into a strong acid. Lakes and forests in many parts of the world have been polluted by **acid rain**.

Fortunately there are other ways of producing the energy we need. We are learning how to generate electricity using wind and wave power. We can now convert sunlight directly into power using solar panels. We are even beginning to use heat from rocks deep inside the Earth to make high pressure steam which drives electric generators.

There is one more source of energy. We have already been using it for hundreds of thousands of years. Half the people in the world rely on it for all their energy needs. It produces as much energy in the USA as nuclear power. It can help reduce the **greenhouse effect** and unlike coal and oil, it is renewable. This energy is **bioenergy** and it is produced from **biomass** – quite simply, plants!

Below *If the problem of pollution like this is to be solved, other sources of energy will have to be used instead.*

PLANT POWERHOUSES

All living things need energy. Animals, ourselves included, obtain that energy directly or indirectly from plants. Some animals feed directly on plants. They are called herbivores, for example cattle, sheep and horses. Others eat the animals that eat the plants. These are called

Below *The energy plants get from the Sun goes to plant-eating animals.*

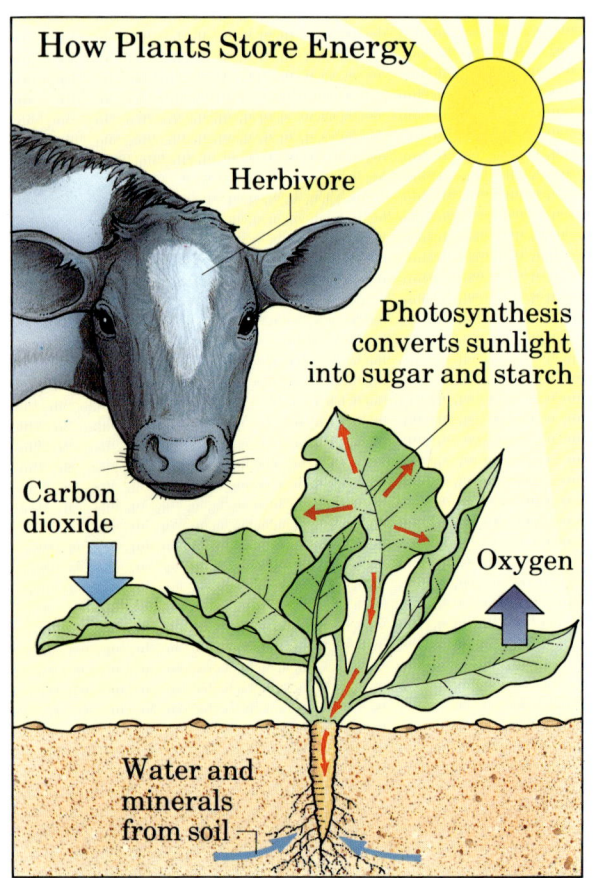

Above *Other animals eat those that eat plants and get energy from them.*

carnivores, for example dogs and cats.

Where do plants obtain their energy from? The answer is that they obtain it directly from the Sun. Plants use the energy in sunlight to make their own food out of carbon, hydrogen and oxygen. The food they make is called carbohydrate, which we recognize as sugar and starch. Having made carbohydrate, a plant then stores it in its leaves, roots or stems for later use. When an animal eats a plant it takes in this stored carbohydrate

8

Sunflowers such as these in a field in Turkey face the Sun, so they can get as much energy from it as possible.

and converts it back into energy to power its own body.

Plants store energy from the Sun. As long as the Sun shines plants will be able to make energy that we can use. This is why they are a good alternative to fossil fuels. They are stores of energy which can be released in several different ways.

As a store of energy a plant can be compared with an electric battery. A battery stores electrical energy, and a plant stores the energy of sunshine. A battery's energy is released when it is part of an electrical circuit with the switch in the 'on' position. It can power model cars, produce light in a torch, or carry out mathematical operations in a calculator. Bioenergy is released not as electrical power, but as heat and light by **combustion**, or burning. It is the heat which is of greatest use to us.

BIOENERGY – THE ANCIENT ALTERNATIVE

Bioenergy has been people's main source of energy for hundreds of thousands of years. It is still the main source of energy for most people in the developing world. Bioenergy is the basis of life itself. *Bios* is the Greek word for life. In the past everybody used bioenergy in the form of a wood fire, for warmth and to cook by. Collecting wood for the fire was an important daily task for everyone – it still is for many people. The forest laws of England which give people the right to collect firewood in Royal Forests were made hundreds of years ago.

Below *These women in India gather wood to use as fuel every day. It provides energy for cooking and keeping warm.*

Above *A Taureg family in North Africa begins the day with tea warmed over a wood fire. This has been done for centuries.*

Making **charcoal** from wood was among the earliest methods of converting biomass into a more **efficient** fuel. Charcoal burns with twice the heat of wood. In Europe charcoal burners used to be found at work in most forests and woodlands.

BIOENERGY – THE ANCIENT ALTERNATIVE

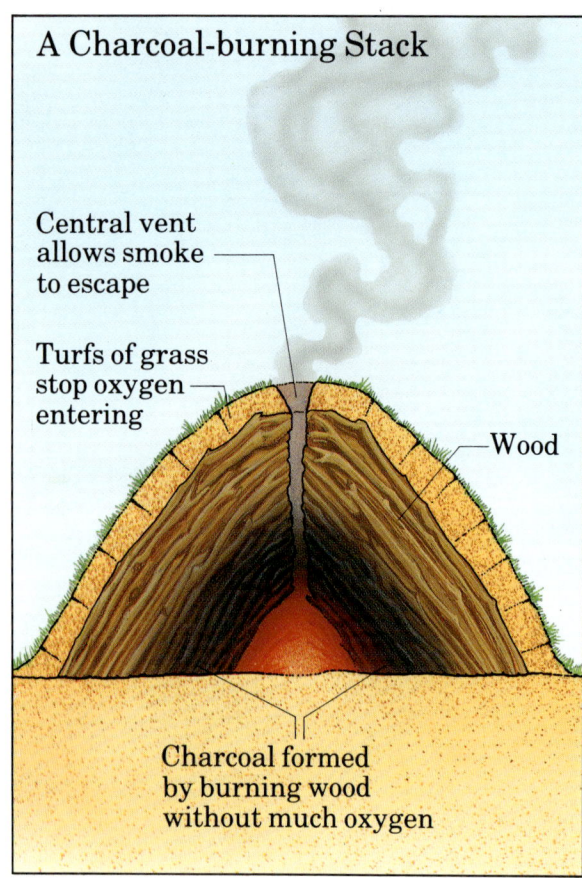

Above *Charcoal burning has been an important way of using biofuel for centuries all around the world.*

Charcoal making is an important industry in much of the developing world. Charcoal is made by burning wood where there is not much air. This can be done by building a stack of logs and branches so that a natural chimney remains through the centre. This stack is then covered in tightly packed earth and set alight at the bottom. Once the stack is burning properly the air holes are blocked and it is left for two to three days.

Wood and charcoal were used to fuel kilns in which pottery was made. Charcoal was used to **smelt** ores that produce metal. Bread ovens were made hot by burning faggots of wood in them. Then the ashes were cleaned out and the bread put in to bake.

Below *This man in China is making charcoal bricks to use as fuel.*

Above *Blacksmiths have always used wood, coal or charcoal to provide them with high enough temperatures to melt metal.*

Blacksmiths used large amounts of charcoal to make tools, weapons and armour. These fuels remained important in **the West** until the beginning of the Industrial Revolution, when the earliest steam engines were powered by wood-fired boilers.

Biofuel has remained an important source of energy in many countries. It is only in the last 200 years or so that the industrialized world has turned more and more to fossil fuels, forgetting in the process how useful biofuels are.

RELEASING BIOENERGY

Biomass is available in many forms. It can be wood, coconut shells, straw, rice husks, sugarcane or even shaped cakes of dried animal dung. The easiest way of releasing the energy contained in such materials is to set fire to it. This has been the traditional use of biofuels for hundreds of thousands of years. It does have some disadvantages, though. First, collecting fuel takes up a lot of time. Second, large dry storage areas have to be built to keep it in. Third, burning biofuels in the open wastes a lot of energy. Most of the heat produced by an open fire in a living room is lost up the chimney.

A fire needs three things to keep it burning. These are fuel, oxygen and heat. Coal and wood are the fuels burned in traditional open fireplaces. As the fuel burns, heat spreads out into the room. This causes the air in the room to become warm. But it is this same warm air which supplies the oxygen to keep the fire burning.

Below *Biofuels can be fun, as well as useful. Bonfires such as this one in Sweden are common throughout the world.*

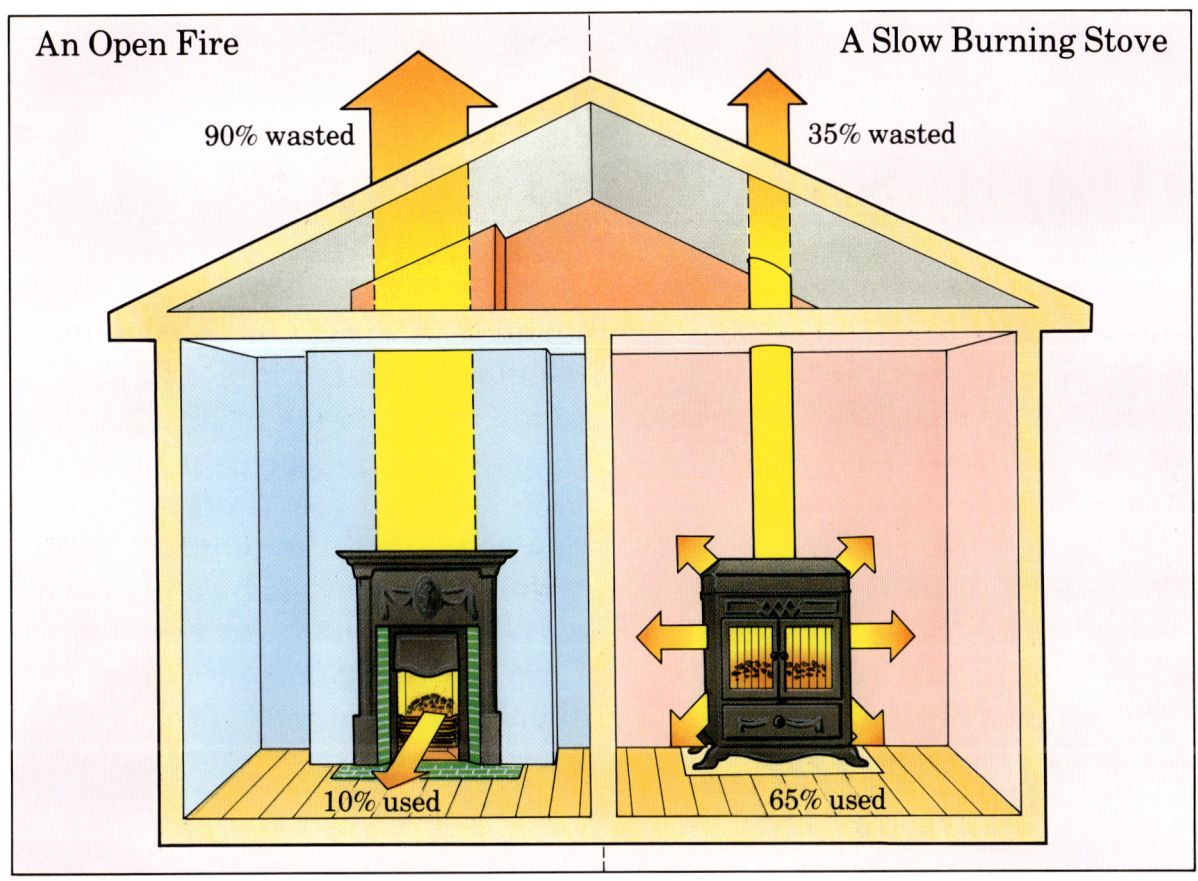

Above *Open fires look good, but waste a lot more heat than sealed stoves. Most of their energy goes up the chimney.*

The warm air is drawn from the room, through the fire and then escapes up the chimney. It then has to be replaced.

The warm air is replaced by cold air drawn from outside the building through gaps in windows and doors. In this way cold draughts are created. More fuel has to be burned to warm the cold air that has been drawn into the room. Some open fires draw their air directly from the outside through underfloor ducts. But heat is still lost up the chimney.

Sealed slow combustion stoves stop much of the heat loss up the chimney. Vents can be opened and closed to control the amount of air taken in. Slow combustion stoves waste less warm air than ordinary fires. Because of this, they need less fuel to heat up a room. The first successful stove of this type was built in America in 1836. Modern designs not only provide room heating, but can also supply hot water for radiators and washing. Many also have an inbuilt oven and hotplates for cooking.

BIOMASS INTO OTHER FUELS

There are four fuels biomass can be converted into. The first is charcoal (see page 11). The others are roasted wood, gas and a liquid fuel similar to petrol.

Roasted wood

A new alternative to charcoal is roasted wood. To make roasted wood, logs are chopped into chips about 5 cm long. These are then dried and roasted in a kiln at a temperature of about 300°C. Roasted wood is a cleaner and more efficient fuel than charcoal and so reduces the number of trees which need to be cut down each year. A factory at Laval de Cere in France now produces about 10,000 tonnes of roasted wood each year.

Below *Most of the wood these lumberjacks are cutting will be used for building, but it could also be used as fuel.*

Gas from roasted wood

The process of manufacturing roasted wood produces gas. If the temperature in the kiln is increased to about 1,500°C and oxygen is pumped in, large amounts of gas can be produced. This gas can then be used to power engines which drive electric generators. This process, called **gasification**, is not new. Petrol and diesel were hard to get during the Second World War. Many trucks were converted to run on gas produced from biofuels. Some even had their own gas generators built on to them. As well as having an exhaust from the engine, they had a tall smoking chimney.

Above *The wood chips that are used to make roasted wood.*

Below *Harold Bate, a UK inventor who runs his car on biogas.*

BIOMASS INTO OTHER FUELS

Gas from waste

Gas can be made in other ways from other materials, notably sewage and waste. Gases are given off when anything **organic** dies and decomposes. One of these gases is **methane**, which is **flammable** and can be used as a fuel. The things at work in decomposition are bacteria. To work properly these bacteria must be in a warm and airless environment.

Biogas digesters are designed to create these conditions. A digester is made up of a tank into which sewage or sorted garbage is pumped. It may be necessary to heat this mixture to the correct temperature, or to put the bacteria that produce the gas into the tank. The bacteria then digest the organic matter, giving off methane in the process. The methane is then carried through pipes to a gasholder. This may be another tank, or a giant plastic balloon. This gas can be used as it is, or it can be used to drive generators that produce electricity. A further advantage of producing biogas in this way is that the solid waste left in the digester makes an excellent fertilizer for food crops.

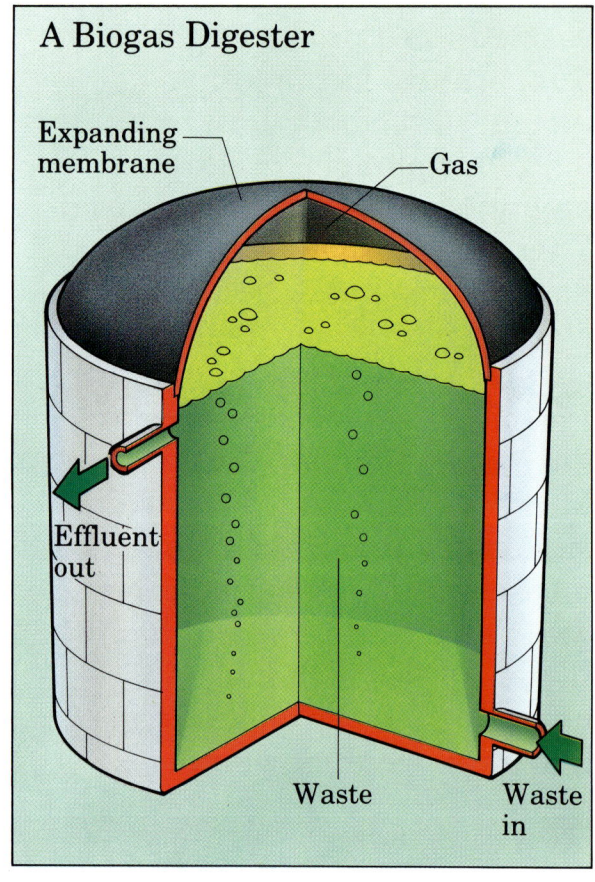

Above *One type of small scale biogas digester. There are many others.*

Biogas digesters are already an important source of energy in a number of countries. This form of bioenergy is particularly useful to small farming communities. This is because they have large amounts of animal dung and other organic wastes available. India and China were among the first countries to build small scale biogas digesters, but they were not very successful at first.

Above *This biogas digester produces methane gas from cattle manure. The gas provides the farm with energy.*

Now, however, China has some 4.5 million working digesters. India has about 30 large scale plants supplying large communities across the country, and thousands of small ones.

BIOMASS INTO OTHER FUELS

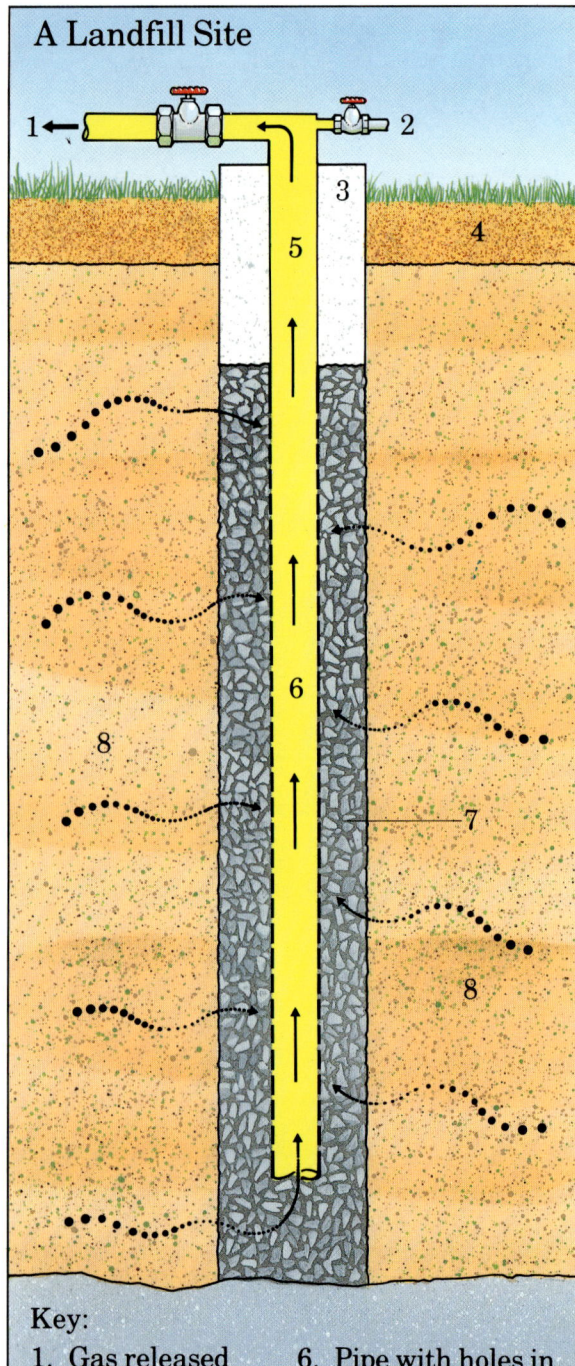

Key:
1. Gas released
2. Gas testing valve
3. Cement
4. Landfill cap
5. Pipe
6. Pipe with holes in, to let in gas
7. Stone chippings that gas passes through
8. Waste

Landfill sites

Biogas is also produced in large amounts at public waste disposal sites. These are large holes in the ground that are filled with waste. That is why they are called landfill sites. These sites receive large amounts of household and industrial rubbish every day. When the sites are full they are sealed with earth and clay. The methane which forms as the rubbish decays is trapped underground. Under these conditions there is a risk of a serious explosion taking place.

To reduce the risk of an explosion and because landfill gas is a useful fuel, engineers now drill into large landfill sites to remove the gas. This gas is sold to factories which use it for many purposes.

The first site to sell its gas was at Palos Verdes in California, where the gas was used to power electric generators. Now there are over 80 landfill sites in the USA producing gas. The UK has fewer landfill sites supplying gas, but the number is increasing. At Stewartby in

Left *A landfill site.*

20

Bedfordshire, for example, bricks are fired in kilns fuelled with landfill gas. Large diesel engines that use gas from the same site drive generators which supply electricity to nearby homes.

Below *A landfill site in the UK. After it has been covered and gas has built up under the surface, it will be possible to use the gas as fuel.*

BIOMASS INTO OTHER FUELS

Running cars on biofuel

Liquid fuel can be made from biomass which has a high sugar content. This is done by fermenting it to produce alcohol. **Fermentation** is the process whereby yeasts digest sugar as food and make alcohol as a waste product. This is what happens when beers and wines are made. Sugar in large amounts comes

Above *A car in Brazil being filled with 'alcool', a form of gasohol.*

from plants such as sugar-cane, sugar beet, cereals, wood and even seaweed. After harvest, the sugar is taken out of these plants, usually by crushing them. Yeast is added to the sugar solution and after several days the sugar has been converted to alcohol. The alcohol is then taken out of the solution.

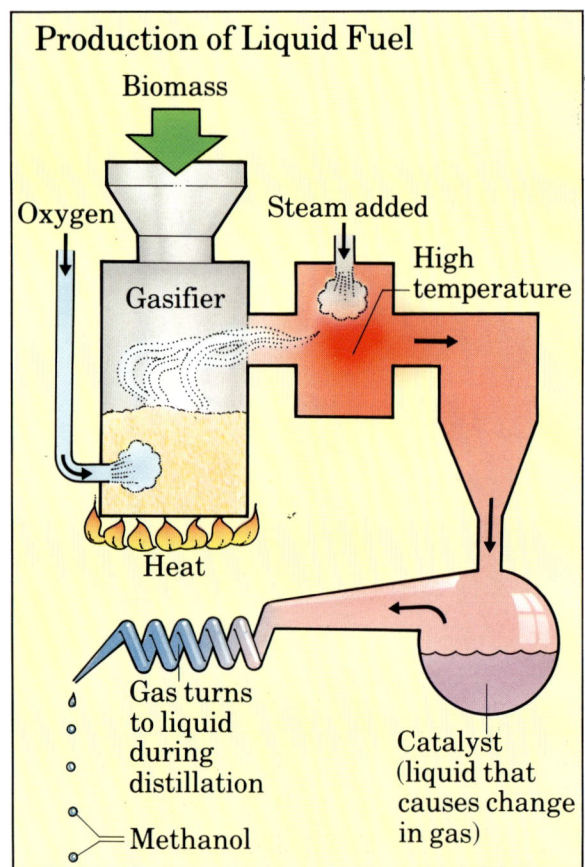

Above *Liquid fuel can be made from sugar cane, wood or even seaweed.*

The alcohol can be added to petrol. In the USA about 30 per cent of petrol sold already has

Above *A crop of sugar-cane in Martinique, in the Caribbean. The sugar-cane could be used to make fuel for cars*

some alcohol added to it. But it is in Brazil that the greatest effort has been made to produce alcohol as fuel. Sugar-cane is grown as a fuel crop there. A factory at São Paulo makes about 1.2 million litres of alcohol each day. However, alcohol is an expensive fuel to make and ways have to be found of reducing the costs involved.

Other crops which have a high oil content can also supply liquid fuels for diesel engines. These include soya, coconut, palms and sunflowers. These are crushed to squeeze out their oil content. This oil can then be used in diesel engines without any further processing and is used to power trucks, tractors and electricity generators.

BIOENERGY IN ACTION

Much work still needs to be done to improve the efficiency of biofuels and to reduce the cost of their manufacture. But there are many examples of biofuels already in use on a large scale.

In Puerto Rico the Bacardi Corporation has built the largest digester for producing biogas in the world. This digester treats about 14,000 kg of factory waste each day and produces 42,500

Below *Although biofuels have been used on a small scale in the past, as shown here, large scale projects are now being built.*

Above *This factory in Brazil produces alcohol from sugar cane. The alcohol is used to fuel cars instead of petrol.*

cubic metres of gas. The gas is used in boilers in the factory and supplies about 40 per cent of their energy needs. A second digester is being built by Bacardi. This means that not only will they be able to supply all their own energy needs, but they will also have some fuel left to sell to other people.

BIOENERGY IN ACTION

Above *This picture shows a biogas digester in the background and a storage tank in the foreground.*

A smaller but equally efficient digester is in operation in Wales at the South Caernarvon Creameries. The digester there uses a by-product of making dairy foods to produce biogas. Since building the digester the company has saved thousands of pounds in energy costs each year.

In addition to this the waste from the digester after it has been processed is clean enough to discharge into a nearby river without causing dangerous pollution. Not only is this digester saving the company large sums of money, but it is friendly to the environment too.

Sometimes landfill sites are not available for the disposal of refuse. Often it can be burned to heat boilers instead. In Sumner County, Tennessee, USA, a refuse-fuelled power plant burns about 100 tonnes of waste each day. The heat generated is used to produce steam, which drives a turbine to produce electricity. Similar furnaces in the UK use refuse as fuel to make cement, or to provide hot water for local homes. Sheffield in the UK has been supplying heat from burning refuse to many homes for several years. There are plans to heat more homes in this way with the help of a firm of heating engineers from Finland.

As well as in Brazil, alcohol as a fuel for cars is produced in both Malawi and Zimbabwe. It is mixed with petrol and called 'gasohol'. This is used in several parts of Africa and is available at ordinary filling stations in the same way that petrol is.

As the amount of fossil fuel left decreases we will come to depend more and more on biomass for energy. A number of poorer countries have created an organization called the Biomass Users Network to research ways of making biofuels from a variety of crops. They see these crops as a way to protect the environment and make use of land that food crops will not grow on.

Below *Household waste can be used to provide power in homes.*

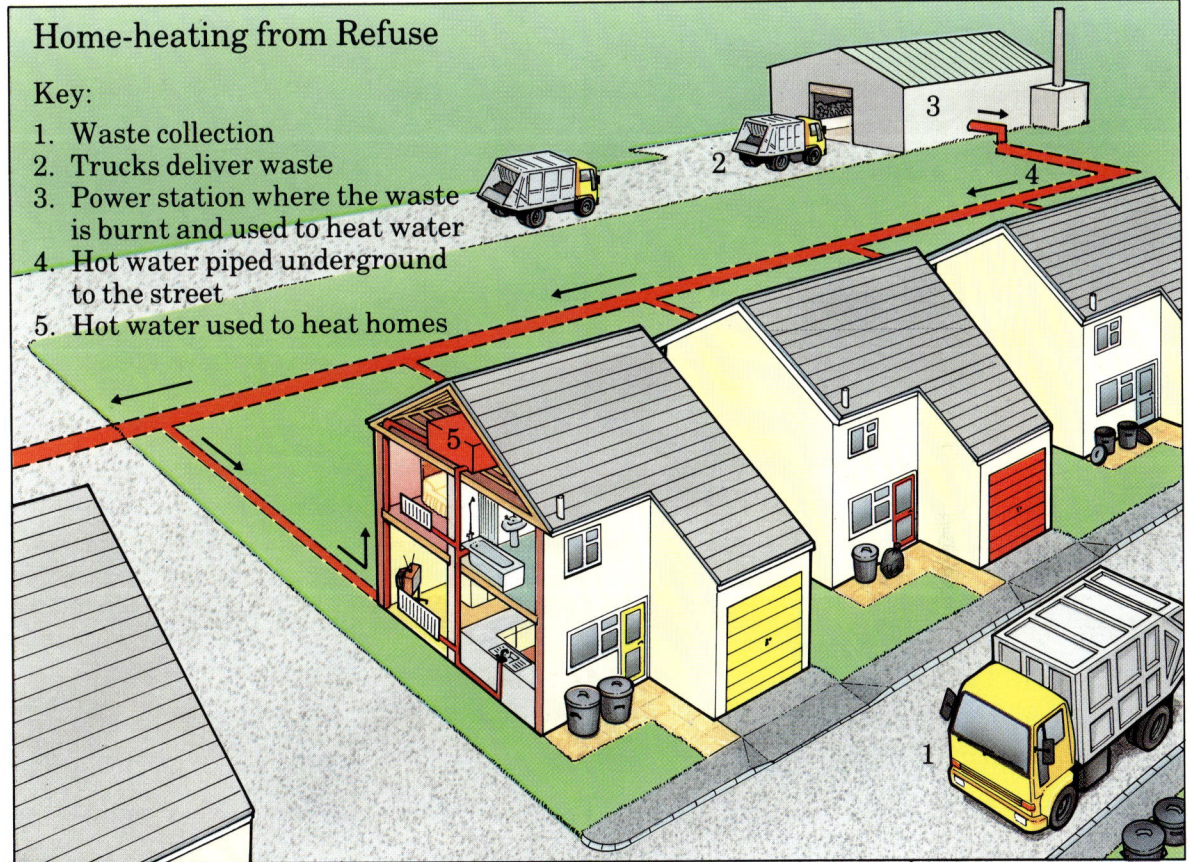

Home-heating from Refuse

Key:
1. Waste collection
2. Trucks deliver waste
3. Power station where the waste is burnt and used to heat water
4. Hot water piped underground to the street
5. Hot water used to heat homes

PROJECT

You will need:

- 2 tablespoons of dried yeast
- 2 tablespoons of sugar
- A balloon
- A small plastic soft drinks bottle
- A plastic thermometer
- Some warm water

How to build your project:

1 Tip the dried yeast and the sugar into the plastic bottle.

2 Pour in the warm water. Water from a tap will be as warm as you need.

3 Cover the top of the bottle with your hand and shake it as hard as you can.

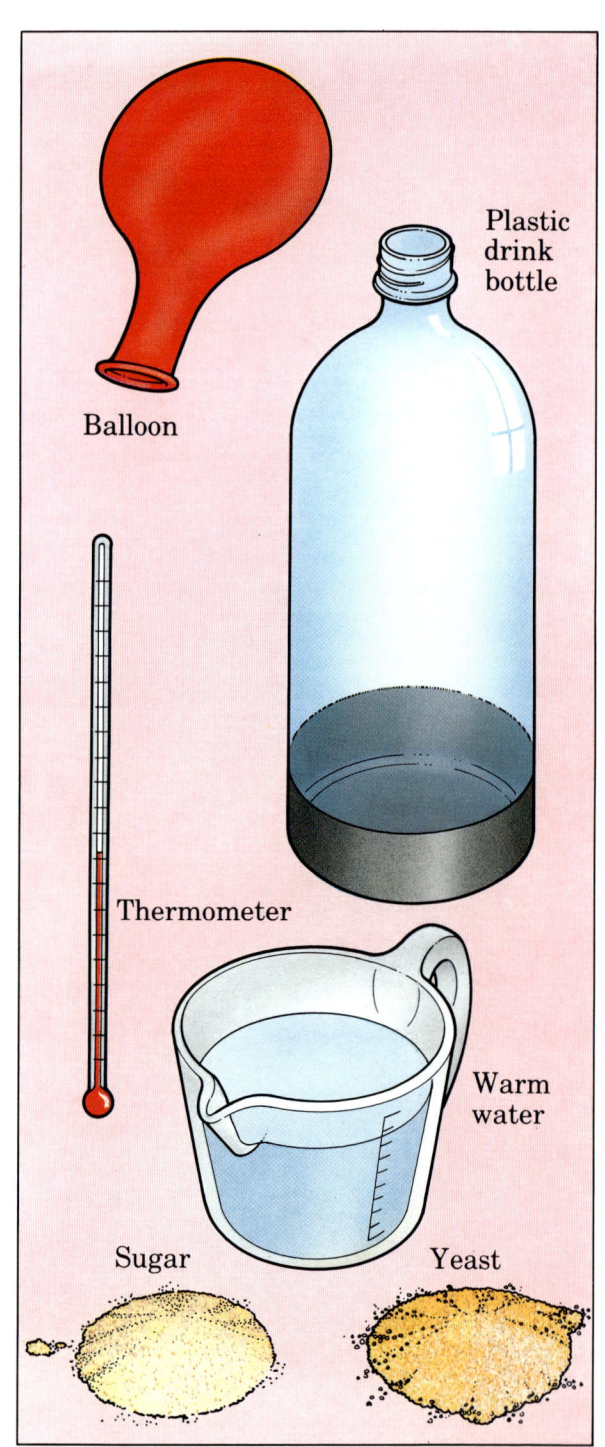

4 Put the balloon over the top of the bottle. If you leave it for an hour, the balloon will have begun to fill up with gas.

5 Try the same experiment with water of different temperatures. Measure the temperature of the water using the thermometer. Which is quickest at filling up the balloon, cold, warm or hot water?

Below *The balloon on top of the bottle will expand in the same way as a biogas store.*

Note:

The balloon fills up with gas in the same way as a storage tank for biogas does. The thing that makes the gas is the yeast. The yeast eats the sugar and gives off gas as a result. Do you remember the biogas digester which had waste poured in, where the waste was eaten by the bacteria which produced gas? This project is meant to show a similar thing in action. From the result of your comparison of different temperatures, can you guess at what temperature the bacteria would work best?

Glossary

Acid rain: Rain which contains pollutant gases from industry, for example sulphur dioxide and nitric oxide. These gases make water strongly acid.

Bioenergy: The energy of living things; energy we obtain from biofuel.

Biofuel: A fuel obtained from biomass (plants).

Biogas: A flammable mixture of gases (mainly methane) given off during the decay of organic matter.

Biomass: Plants and parts of plants.

Charcoal: A fuel produced by burning wood in a restricted air supply.

Combustion: Burning. Heat and light are usually produced during combustion.

Efficiency: The work done, or heat, light, etc. created by a certain measured amount of energy. Less energy used to produce an effect means greater efficiency in the energy-using system.

Fermentation: The conversion of sugar and starch to alcohol by the action of yeast.

Flammable: Something which burns easily is known as being flammable, for example paper, wood and some gases.

Fossil fuels: Coal, oil and natural gas. The remains of plants and animals that lived millions of years ago.

Gasification: The production of gas from wood by heating it under pressure.

Greenhouse effect: The warming of the Earth through the production of gases which trap the Sun's heat.

Greenhouse gas: A gas which traps the Sun's heat – carbon dioxide and methane for example.

Methane: A flammable gas produced by the decay of organic matter.

Organic: Plants and animals.

Pollution: The contamination of our surroundings with toxic or poisonous waste.

Smelt: To heat rock in order to remove metal from it.

The West: The richest parts of the world, mainly Europe and North America.

Picture acknowledgements

Artwork by Nick Hawken.

The publishers would like to thank the following for supplying photographs: David Bowden 12; Environmental Picture Library *cover*, 6, 11, 24; Energy Technology Support Unit 26; Eye Ubiquitous 9; Geoscience Features 23; Hutchison 4, 19, 21, 25; Photri 8, 16; Christine Osborne 10; Topham/Associated Press 14, 17; Zefa 7, 13, 22.

Further information

Australia

The Energy Information Centre
139 Flinders Street
Melbourne 3000

Canada

Energy, Mines and Resources
580 Booth Street
Ottawa KIA OE4

UK

Renewable Energy Enquiries
  Bureau
Energy Technology Support Unit
Building 156
Harwell Laboratory
Oxford OX11 ORA

Council for Environmental
  Education
School of Education
University of Reading
London Road
Reading RG1 5AQ

The Centre for Alternative
  Technology
Llwyngern Quarry
Machynllech
Wales

Network for Alternative
  Technology and Technology
  Assessment
Faculty of Technology
Open University
Milton Keynes MK7 6AA

USA

Energy Technology Department
US Department of Energy
1000 Independence Avenue
Washington
DC 20585

Books to read

For children:
Conserving Our Atmosphere,
  J Baines (Wayland, 1989)
Energy and Natural Resources,
  G Houghton & J Wakefield
  (MacMillan)
Energy Without End, M Flood
  (Friends of the Earth, 1986)
Fun With Science, Brenda
  Walpole (Kingfisher, 1988)
Our Future Needs, N Ardley
  (Franklin Watts, 1982)
*The Young Scientist Book of
  Electricity*, P Chapman
  (Usborne, 1989)

For teachers:
Biomass as Fuel, LP White &
  LG Plaskett (Academic Press,
  1981)
*Energy, Power Sources and
  Electricity*, P Neal (Dryad, 1988)
Grow Your Own Energy, M Cross
(Blackwell, 1984)

Index

Page numbers in **bold** refer to pictues and text. Others refer only to text.

Bioenergy, sources of
  lumberjacks **23**
  sugar cane **23**
Bioenergy, useage of
  bonfires **14**
  digesters **18**, **19**
  fireplaces **15**
  slow combustion stoves **15**
  Taureg **11**
Biofuel and
  carnivores **8**
  herbivores **8**
  photosynthesis **8**
Biofuel, forms of
  charcoal 11, **12**
  gas **17–21**
  gasohol 22
  roasted wood 16, **17**

Greenhouse effect **5**, 7
Greenhouse gas 5

Landfill sites **20**, **21**
Large scale bioenergy users
  Bacardi Corporation 24
  Brazil **25**
  Sheffield Council 27
  South Caernvarvon Creameries 26